THE UNOFFICIAL GUIDE TO THE EUROVISION SONG CONTEST IN MALMO 2024

BILLY SHEARS

EIGHTH DAY MUSIC PUBLISHING

Copyright 2024 by Billy Shears

No portion of this book may be reproduced in any form without written permission from the publisher or author, except as permitted by U.K. copyright law.

Contents

1. INTRODUCTION - MALMO, 2024   2
2. TIMELINE   6
3. THE MALMO ARENA   9
4. PARTICIPANTS IN THE CONTEST   17
5. SONG ENTRANT DETAILS BY COUNTRY   19
6. OLLY ALEXANDER   24
7. FIVE THINGS TO DO AND SEE IN MALMO   26
8. MALMO BAR CULTURE   30
9. GENERAL ESSENTIAL INFORMATION   32

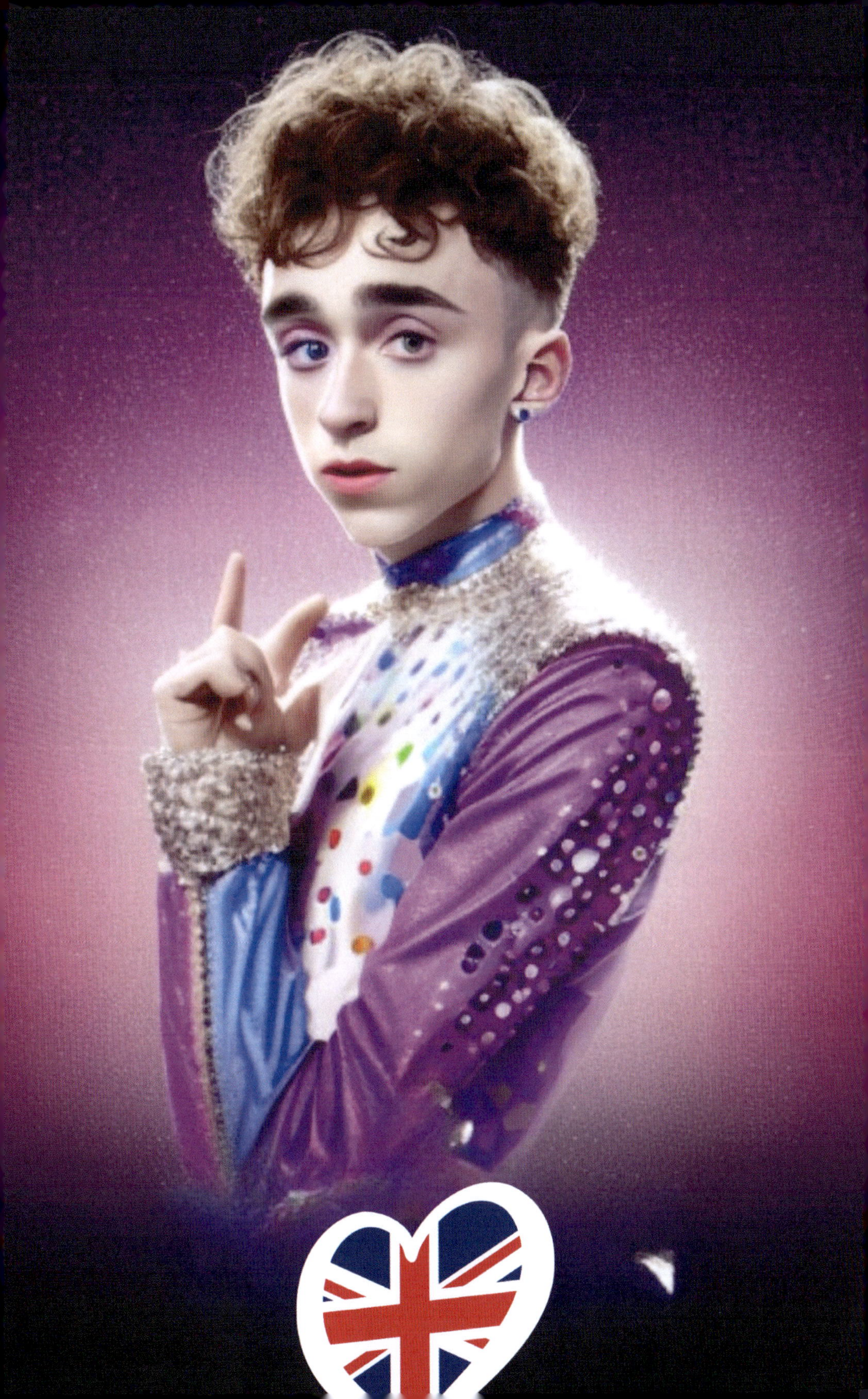

EUROVISION SONG CONTEST
MALMÖ 2024

The highly anticipated Grand Final of the Eurovision Song Contest 2024 is set to unfold at the illustrious Malmö Arena on Saturday, 11th May, accompanied by riveting Semi-Finals on Tuesday, 7th May, and Thursday, 9th May. The orchestration of this spectacular event rests in the capable hands of the Swedish broadcaster SVT, in collaboration with the esteemed European Broadcasting Union (EBU). The genesis of this honourable responsibility can be traced back to Loreen's historic triumph in Liverpool in 2023, paving the way for Sweden to host the Eurovision Song Contest once again.

The selection of Malmö as the hosting city for this grandiose musical extravaganza stems from a rigorous city bid process. This comprehensive evaluation scrutinised the venue's facilities, its capacity to seamlessly accommodate throngs of visiting delegations, crew members, fans, and journalists, as well as the city's overall infrastructure and adherence to various criteria. Malmö's triumphant bid makes it the third occasion the city has been bestowed with the prestigious task of hosting the Eurovision Song Contest, with previous editions gracing its stage in 1992 and 2013. Notably, this marks a departure from the convention of choosing capital cities, making it the first time in five consecutive Contests that the Eurovision Song Contest will not be held in a nation's capital.

Sweden, a nation with a rich Eurovision history, will be hosting the event for the seventh time in 2024. In addition to the upcoming spectacle in Malmö, Sweden has previously welcomed the Eurovision Song Contest in Stockholm in 1975,

2000, and 2016, as well as in Gothenburg in 1985. These occurrences underscore Sweden's enduring commitment to showcasing and celebrating the diversity of European music on the global stage. The anticipation for the 2024 edition is palpable, as the Eurovision Song Contest once again takes centre stage in this culturally vibrant and musically rich Scandinavian nation.

"We are proud and happy to welcome the Eurovision Song Contest to Malmö again", said Katrin Stjernfeldt Jammeh, chairman of the city's municipal executive board.

Eurovision Song Contest Executive Supervisor Martin Österdahl welcomed the news:

"The EBU is thrilled that Malmö has been selected as the Host City for the Eurovision Song Contest 2024. Malmö holds a special place in the history of the Contest, having successfully hosted it firstly in 1992 and then in 2013 - following Loreen's last win.

We're excited to be returning to this vibrant and dynamic city which has demonstrated it has the venues and infrastructure that are perfect for staging the world's largest live music event.

Malmö's commitment to diversity, inclusivity, and innovation aligns perfectly with the spirit of the competition. Furthermore, its compact size and well-developed transport infrastructure means everyone involved in the Contest, including delegations, media, and fans will be able to navigate the city easily.

Its commitment to sustainability and green initiatives also aligns perfectly with our own values, making it an ideal Host City for the 68th Eurovision Song Contest.

Malmö's bid demonstrated a huge passion for the Eurovision Song Contest, and I have full confidence in their ability to create an unforgettable experience that will bring together fans, artists, and viewers across the globe. Together with Host Broadcaster SVT, we will create an extraordinary celebration of music, unity, and diversity that will captivate the world in May next year."

Ebba Adielsson, Executive Producer for SVT added:

"When we finally had all the options, we did an overall assessment to consider all factors involved in organizing this huge event. Malmö was eventually chosen as it met all the criteria and provides a location with great venues and is a city where all those attending the Eurovision Song Contest can move around easily. Malmö is also firmly committed to providing both those visiting and living in the city a chance to participate in the festivities."

In the heart of Scandinavia, the city of Malmö is poised to become the epicentre of musical brilliance as it hosts the Eurovision Song Contest in 2024. With a rich history of successful events, Sweden once again opens its arms to the Eurovision family, promising a celebration of diversity, creativity, and unforgettable performances.

The honour of hosting the Eurovision Song Contest was bestowed upon Malmö following Sweden's impressive victory in Liverpool in 2023, where Loreen's historic win paved the way for the nation to take the reins of this prestigious musical extravaganza. It marks the seventh time that Sweden will play host, with Malmö having previously hosted in 1992 and 2013.

One notable departure from tradition is Malmö's selection as the host city, deviating from the customary choice of capital cities. This decision adds a unique flavour to the event, making it the first time in five consecutive Contests that the Eurovision Song Contest will not grace a nation's capital. Malmö's selection signifies a nod to the city's capabilities, infrastructure, and commitment to delivering a memorable experience.

Malmö's journey to becoming the Eurovision host city was no easy feat. The city underwent a rigorous bid process, demonstrating its prowess in various aspects, from state-of-the-art venue facilities to the ability to accommodate thousands of visitors, including delegations, crew, fans, and journalists. The city's infrastructure, hospitality, and adherence to specified criteria clinched its victory, earning Malmö the honour of hosting the Eurovision Song Contest once again.

The Malmö Arena, the chosen venue for the Grand Final and Semi-Finals, is no stranger to Eurovision glory. Having hosted the event in 1992 and 2013, the arena is imbued with a sense of Eurovision history, and its stage is set to witness yet another spectacular showcase of musical talent from across Europe.

The Eurovision Song Contest has long been celebrated as a platform for cultural exchange and diversity. As Malmö welcomes delegations from various nations, the city is gearing up to embrace the global melting pot of music, where genres, languages, and artistic expressions converge on one stage. The vibrancy of Malmö and its cultural richness promise to add an extra layer of excitement to this year's festivities.

As the anticipation builds and Malmö prepares to showcase its prowess as the host city, the Eurovision Song Contest 2024 is poised to be a harmonious celebration of music, unity, and cultural diversity. With the historic Malmö Arena as its stage, this edition promises to be a memorable chapter in the Eurovision legacy, leaving an indelible mark on the hearts of fans worldwide. The countdown has begun, and Malmö is ready to welcome the world to a musical spectacle like no other.

TIMELINE OF THE EVENT

Eurovision Song Contest — Malmö 2024

First Semi-Final
Tuesday, 07 May, 2024, 21:00 CEST

Second Semi-Final
Thursday, 09 May, 2024, 21:00 CEST

Grand Final
Saturday, 11 May, 2024, 21:00 CEST

Venue & Location
Malmö Arena, Malmö, Sweden

February 2024

Friday 16 February

   Germany: Eurovision Song Contest – Das Deutsche Finale, 22:20)

Saturday 17 February

   Denmark: Melodi Grand Prix, 20:00
   Estonia: Eesti Laul final, 18:30
   Iceland: Söngvakeppnin semi-final 1, 20:45
   Lithuania: Eurovizija.LT final, 20:00
   Moldova: Etapa Națională, 18:00
   Sweden: Melodifestivalen semi-final 3, 20:00

Thursday 22 February

   Croatia: Dora semi-final 1

Friday 23 February

   Croatia: Dora semi-final 2

Saturday 24 February

   Iceland: Söngvakeppnin semi-final 2, 20:45
   Portugal: Festival da Canção semi-final 1, 22:00
   San Marino: Una Voce per San Marino final
   Sweden: Melodifestivalen semi-final 4, 20:00)

Sunday 25 February

   Croatia: Dora final

Tuesday 27 February

   Serbia: Pesma za Evroviziju semi-final 1

Thursday 29 February

   Serbia: Pesma za Evroviziju semi-final 2

March 2024

Saturday 02 March

   Iceland: Söngvakeppnin final
   Portugal: Festival da Canção semi-final 2
   Serbia: Pesma za Evroviziju final
   Sweden: Melodifestivalen semi-final 5

Saturday 09 March

Portugal: Festival da Canção final
Sweden: Melodifestivalen final

April 2024

TBA
  TBA

May 2024

Tuesday 7 May - 21:00 CEST
  Eurovision Song Contest, First Semi-Final live from Malmö, Sweden
Thursday 9 May - 21:00 CEST
  Eurovision Song Contest, Second Semi-Final live from Malmö, Sweden
Saturday 11 May - 21:00 CEST
  Eurovision Song Contest, Grand Final live from Malmö, Sweden

All dates and times subject to change.

THE MALMO ARENA

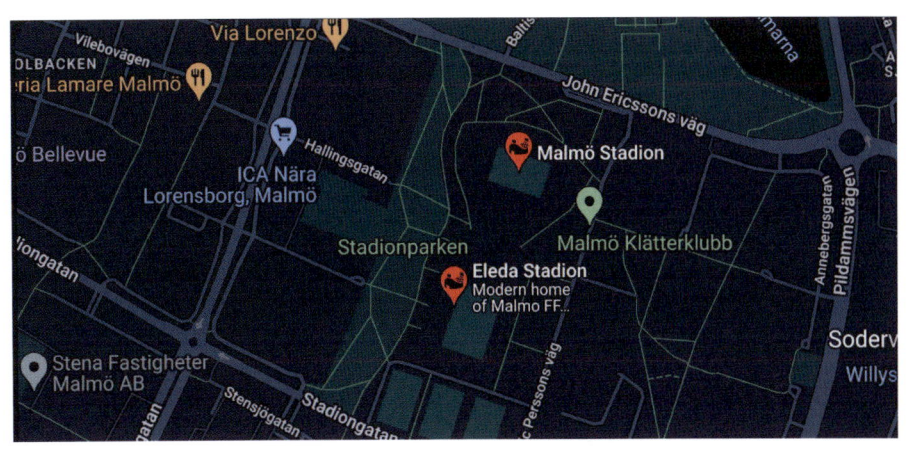

The genesis of the Hyllie district's development in Malmö traces back to the initiation of plans for a new railway station in the area. Percy Nilsson, the visionary behind Malmö Arena, embarked on a meticulous planning process for a super-arena situated in Hyllie. This ambitious endeavour materialized with the unwavering support and cooperation of the City of Malmö.

In 2001, the City of Malmö prioritized Hyllie as its key urban development zone. Steen & Ström, a leading shopping centre development company in Scandinavia, secured construction rights for a shopping centre, residential areas, and offices. Their local development plan gained formal municipal approval in February 2006. Commencing construction in February 2008, Steen & Ström worked on the Emporia Shopping Centre, slated for completion in February-March 2012.

The green light for Malmö Arena's construction came in September 2006, and the groundbreaking ceremony took place on 10 January 2007. In 2007, the City of Malmö determined the arena's name, with naming rights held by the city for an initial period of 5 + 5 years.

The grand inauguration of Malmö Arena unfolded on 6-7 November 2008, marked by a spectacular performance titled "The Swedish Music Wonder." This milestone rectified a longstanding issue for Malmö, as the absence of a suitable arena had previously hindered the town from hosting major touring shows and concerts. With the establishment of Malmö Arena, this deficiency has been definitively addressed, opening the doors to a new era of cultural and entertainment opportunities for the vibrant city.

One thing noting – the arena is a CASH-FREE ARENA

Of course, most types of payment and credit cards work. For all sums under 200 SEK you do not even need to enter any code. Simply insert or "flip" the card and approve the purchase.

ARENA BARS

DIAMOND BAR

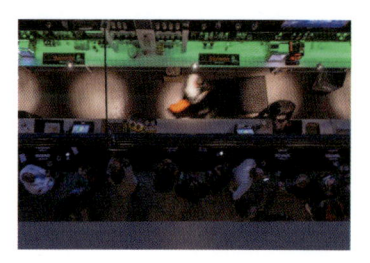

Malmö Arena's largest bar! The perfect place for a drink or beer before the event. The bars are located on the ground floor at section A14-A17, at a comfortable distance to kiosks and fast food outlets.

SPORTBAREN BAR

Simple, relaxed atmosphere with two bars that are fully licensed. The Sports Bar is on the ground floor at section A10-A11.#

MEZZANIN BAR

En Trappa Upp has plenty of seats and views of Hyllie Boulevard. The bar is located in the West Foyer on the ground floor at section A5–A6.

TJECK BAR & ICE BAR

There are two bars at the Malmö Arena D level. The Tjeck Bar is located at section D26–D27 and the Ice Bar at section D30–D31. These bars are open for selected events and are close to the stands!

KIOSK & FAST FOOD

Malmö Arena Express conists of 24 kiosks located around the Arena. The kiosks and fast food offer hot food such as hamburgers and sausages as well as a wide range of drinks, snacks and candy!
  Vegetarian and gluten-free options are always offered.
  Kiosks and fast food are open in connection with all events.
  *It is not aloud to take food, snacks and drinks into Malmö Arena.

RESTAURANTS

PERCYS RESTAURANG & BAR, MALMÖ ARENA

A unique panoramic view of Malmö Arena, used as an event restaurant as well as conference rooms with a capacity of up to 650 seated dinner guests.

The restaurant serves today's lunch on a buffet during weekdays as well as event menus on selected dates.

A unique panoramic view of Malmö Arena, used as an event restaurant as well as conference rooms with a capacity of up to 650 seated dinner guests.

The restaurant serves today's lunch on a buffet during weekdays as well as event menus on selected dates.

RESTAURANG PALISSAD, MALMÖ ARENA

A flexible restaurant that can be divided into 3 parts and changed shape according to need. The venue is used as well as an event restaurant and conference room with a capacity of up to 1200 seated dinner guests.

The restaurant serves event menus during selected dates.

LOUNGE4, MALMÖ ARENA

On the fourth floor overlooking the entire arena you will find these exclusive seats. Here you can spend time with your company, eat delicious food in the form of light meals and enjoy a large selection of drinks while enjoying Redhawks hockey matches as well as specific events and concerts.

NILSSONS RESTAURANG & BAR, MALMÖ ARENA HOTEL

Serves modern dishes on locally produced ingredients. The restaurant can be found on the entrance floor of the BEST WESTERN Malmö Arena Hotel.

The restaurant serves lunch and evening menu.

SKYBAR @ MALMÖ ARENA HOTEL

Welcome to Malmö's biggest sky bar, 360 degree views, awesome pizzas, fantastic drinks, and sparkling wine.

GETTING TO THE ARENA

Its easy to get to Malmö Arena with both trains and buses.
You will find practical information and routes, as well as maps at his link:https://www.malmoarena.com/en/find-us
There are taxi ranks right alongside Malmö Arena.

GENERAL INFORMATION ABOUT THE ARENA

Smoking is not permitted in Malmö Arena. This also applies to e-cigarettes. For selected events, a special smoking area will be opened. Ask a member of our entrance staff when you are here.

For sporting events and selected concerts/performances, there will be a total of 53 reserved places for spectators in wheelchairs and the same number of places for those accompanying them. For concerts and other events where the stage is relocated, the number of wheelchair places is subject to change. For wheelchair reservations, please call +46 (0)77-578 00 00.
No food or drinks from outside the arena are allowed.
If we consider a person to be too intoxicated, he/she will not be allowed to enter Malmö Arena.
No camera or recording devices and/or selfiesticks are allowed
No pets of any kind are allowed.
Malmö Arena adheres to the authority decision 1/11 regarding a total ban of bags at major public events, this applies to all types of bags regardless of size. This also includes plastic bags, clear and covered. Exceptions may be made for people who for medical reasons need to bring a smaller bag.
Its not allowed to bring scooters or bikes in to the arena, neither the batteries for them.
Before entering the arena, there will be a security check.

MALMO ARENA SEATING PLAN

WHERE ARE YOU SITTING?

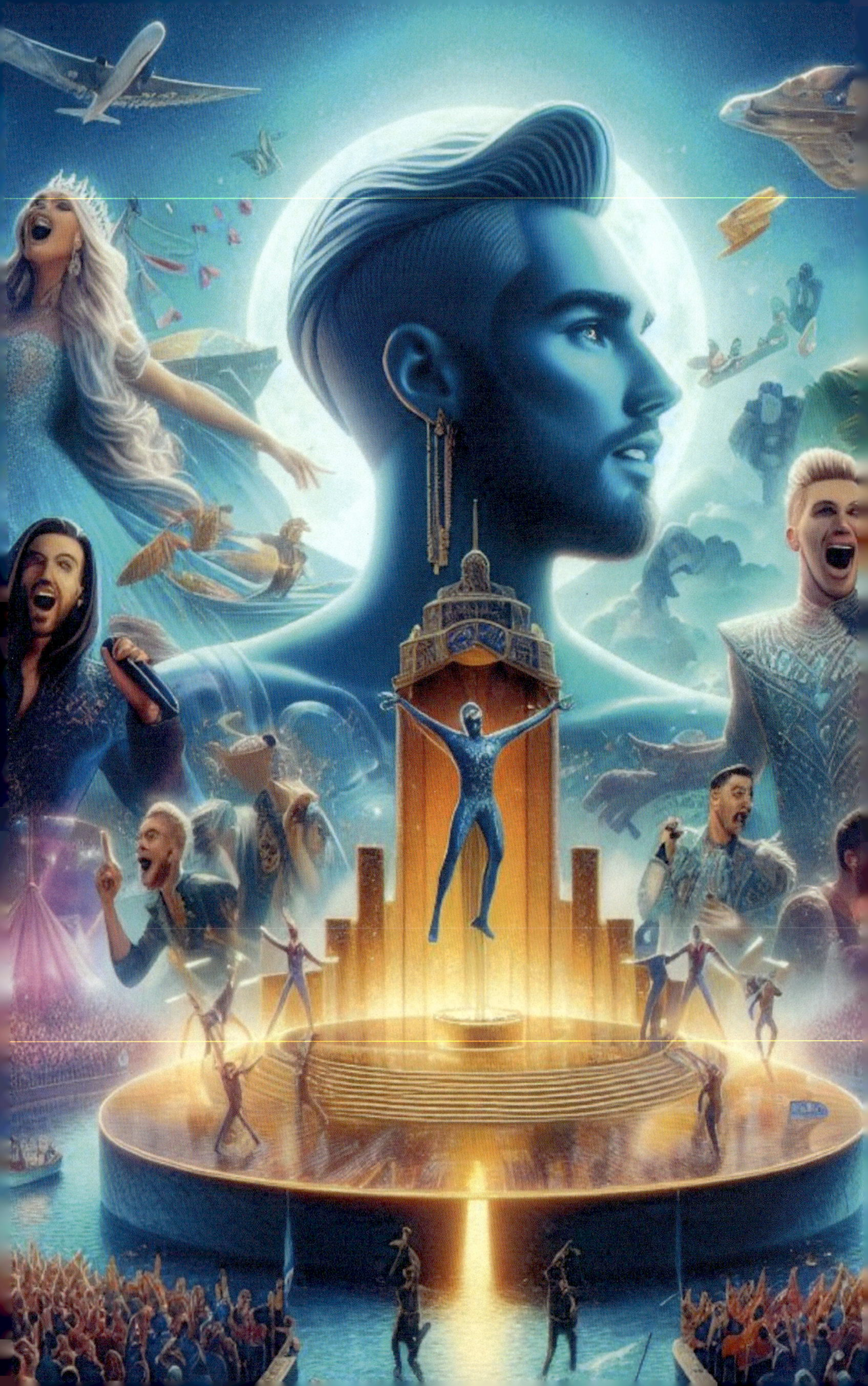

PARTICIPANTS IN THE CONTEST

Participants

37 countries will participate at the Eurovision Song Contest 2024:

Albania	Estonia	Latvia	Serbia
Armenia	Finland	Lithuania	Slovenia
Australia	France	Luxembourg	Spain
Austria	Georgia	Malta	Sweden
Azerbaijan	Germany	Moldova	Switzerland
Belgium	Greece	Netherlands	Ukraine
Croatia	Iceland	Norway	United Kingdom
Cyprus	Ireland	Poland	
Czechia	Israel	Portugal	
Denmark	Italy	San Marino	

Changes from Eurovision 2023

Luxembourg will return to Eurovision after 30 years of absence. Read more.

Romania is the only country from Eurovision 2023 that won't participate in Eurovision 2024.

Who's in which Semi-final?

Last year's winner (Sweden) and the Big-5 countries (Germany, France, Italy, Spain and United Kingdom) are pre-qualified for the Grand Final on 11 May 2024. The rest of the countries were allocated to one of the two Semi-finals that will be held on 7 and 9 May 2024. The allocation draw was made on 30 January.

SEMI-FINAL 1
7 May 2024

FIRST HALF
- Croatia
- Cyprus
- Ireland
- Lithuania
- Poland
- Serbia
- Ukraine

SECOND HALF
- Australia
- Azerbaijan
- Finland
- Iceland
- Luxembourg
- Moldova
- Portugal
- Slovenia

VOTE IN SEMI-FINAL 1:
- Germany
- United Kingdom
- Sweden

SEMI-FINAL 2
9 May 2024

FIRST HALF
- Albania
- Armenia
- Austria
- Czechia
- Denmark
- Greece
- Malta
- Switzerland

SECOND HALF
- Belgium
- Estonia
- Georgia
- Israel
- Latvia
- Netherlands
- Norway
- San Marino

VOTE IN SEMI-FINAL 2:
- Spain
- France
- Italy

SONG ENTRANT DETAILS BY COUNTRY

To be eligible to take part in the Eurovision Song Contest, a country must have a national broadcaster holding an active membership with the EBU, capable of receiving and broadcasting the contest live nationwide through the Eurovision network. Invitations to participate are extended to all EBU members.

On 5 December 2023, the EBU revealed that 37 countries had been confirmed for the 2024 contest. Luxembourg is poised to make a return after a 31-year hiatus since its last involvement in 1993. In contrast, Romania, a participant in the 2023 contest, was initially indicated as not participating in 2024; this was later officially confirmed on 25 January 2024.

All information is correct as of going to press in February 2024, but is obviously liable to change.

Country	Broadcaster	Artist	Song	Language	Songwriter(s)
Albania	RTSH	Besa	"Zemrën n'dorë"	Albanian	- Besa Kokëdhima - Kledi Bahiti - Petrit Sefaj - Rozana Radi
Armenia	AMPTV				
Australia	SBS	TBA 6 March 2024[42]			
Austria	ORF	Kaleen	"We Will Rave"[49]	TBA 1 March 2024[44]	- Jimmy "Joker" Thörnfeldt - TBA[43]
Azerbaijan	İTV				
Belgium	RTBF	Mustii	"Before the Party's Over"[45]	TBA 20 February 2024[45]	
Croatia	HRT	TBD 25 February 2024[46]			
Cyprus	CyBC	Silia Kapsis	"Liar"	TBA 29 February 2024[47]	- Dimitris Kontopoulos - Elke Tiel[48]
Czechia	ČT	Aiko	"Pedestal"	English	- Alena Shirmanova-Kostebelova - Steven Ansell[49]
Denmark	DR	TBD 17 February 2024[50]			
Estonia	ERR	TBD 17 February 2024[51]			

Country	Broadcaster	Artist	Song	Language	Songwriter(s)
Finland	Yle	Windows95man[a][b]	"No Rules!"	English	- Piispanen - Jussi Roine - Teemu Keisteri
France	France Télévisions	Slimane	"Mon amour"	French	- Meïr Salah - Slimane Nebchi - Yaacov Salah[53]
Georgia	GPB	Nutsa Buzaladze			
Germany	NDR[c]	Isaak	"Always on the Run"	English	- Greg Taro - Isaak Guderian - Kevin Lehr - Leo Salminen
Greece	ERT	Marina Satti	"Zari" (Ζάρι)[55]	TBA 7 March 2024[56]	
Iceland	RÚV	TBD 2 March 2024[57]			
Ireland	RTÉ	Bambie Thug	"Doomsday Blue"	English	- Bambie Ray Robinson - Olivia Cassy Brooking - Sam Matlock - Tyler Ryder
Israel	IPBC	Eden Golan	TBA March 2024[58]		
Italy	RAI	Angelina Mango	"La noia"	Italian	- Angelina Mango - Dario Faini

					Calearo
Latvia	LTV	Dons	"Hollow"	English	- Artūrs Šingirejs - Kate Northrop - Liam Geddes
Lithuania	LRT	TBD 17 February 2024[59]			
Luxembourg	RTL	Tali	"Fighter"	French, English	- Ana Zimmer - Dario Faini - Manon Romiti - Silvio Lisbonne
Malta	PBS	Sarah Bonnici	"Loop"	English	- Kevin Lee - Leire Gotxi Angel - Michael Joe Cini - Sarah Bonnici - Sebastian Pritchard-James[60]
Moldova	TRM	TBD 17 February 2024[61]			
Netherlands	AVROTROS	Joost Klein	TBA March 2024[62]	Dutch[63]	- Donny Ellerström - Joost Klein[63]
Norway	NRK	Gåte	"Ulveham"	Norwegian	- Gunnhild Sundli

Country	Broadcaster	Artist	Song	Language	Songwriter(s)
Portugal	RTP	TBD 9 March 2024[65]			
San Marino	SMRTV	TBD 24 February 2024[66]			
Serbia	RTS	TBD 2 March 2024[67]			
Slovenia	RTVSLO	Raiven	"Veronika"	Slovene	- Bojan Cvjetićanin [sl] - Danilo Kapel - Klavdija Kopina - Martin Bezjak - Peter Khoo - Sara Briški Cirman
Spain	RTVE	Nebulossa	"Zorra"	Spanish	- María Bas - Mark Dasousa
Sweden	SVT	TBD 9 March 2024[68]			
Switzerland	SRG SSR	TBA March 2024[69]			
Ukraine	Suspilne	Alyona Alyona and Jerry Heil	"Teresa & Maria"	Ukrainian[d]	- Aliona Savranenko - Anton Chilibi - Ivan Klymenko - Yana Shemaieva
United Kingdom	BBC	Olly Alexander	"Dizzy"	TBA 1 March 2024[71]	- Oliver Alexander Thornton

OLLY ALEXANDER

As he embarks on his latest musical venture, Olly Alexander stands out as a pioneering force in contemporary pop music. The accomplished singer, actor, and fashion icon has carved an impressive path, boasting three highly successful albums that collectively earned him two #1 UK albums and a remarkable 10 UK Top 40 singles. Recently, he was honored with the BRIT Billion Award, a testament to his global impact with 6.5 billion streams.

Transitioning from the group Years & Years to a solo project, 2024 marks the inception of a new era for Olly. His significance transcends the realm of music, notably demonstrated by his involvement in the Russell T Davies show, "It's A Sin," which secured the prestigious Best New Drama accolade at the National Television Awards. Additionally, Olly's performance garnered a nomination for Leading Actor at the 2022 BAFTA Television Awards.

Beyond the music scene, Olly Alexander's influence extends to headlining arenas and festivals worldwide. His collaborations with esteemed artists such as Sir Elton John, Kylie, and Pet Shop Boys further underscore his versatility and broad appeal. Recently enshrined at Madame Tussauds London, Olly's wax figure solidifies his icon-status, a recognition well-deserved for a pop sensation who has played a pivotal role in reshaping British culture.

In a remarkable development, Olly now steps onto the Eurovision Song Contest stage, representing the United Kingdom. His multifaceted career, encompassing music, acting, and fashion, positions him as a unique and influential voice, leaving an indelible mark on the entertainment landscape.

Euro♡ision
SONG CONTEST

FIVE THINGS TO DO AND SEE IN MALMO

Malmo is also known for **its modern setting, including a twisting skyscraper and an award-winning library**. If you are looking for cultural experiences in Malmo, there are dozens of museums dedicated to art, natural history, and the sea.

1. MALMO CASTLE

Malmo Castle was built in 1434, and is one of Sweden's oldest surviving Renaissance castles. Surrounded by a moat and lush gardens, the restored fortress houses the Malmo City Museum, Science and Maritime House, and the Natural History Museum, among others. There's also the *U3* submarine that was used during the Second World War, which you can explore on your own or by joining a guided tour. Admission to Malmo Castle is free for those younger than 20 years old, making it a great place to visit for families.

2. STORTORGER SQUARE

Commencing your exploration of Malmo from Stortorget Square is an excellent choice, given its proximity to some of the city's oldest and most captivating landmarks. The pedestrian streets surrounding the square are adorned with historic buildings, providing a visual journey into Malmo's past. At the heart of Stortorget Square, an equestrian sculpture of King Karl X Gustav, erected in 1540, adds a regal touch to the ambiance.

Adjacent to the square, you'll find noteworthy landmarks, including Apoteket Lejone, Sweden's oldest pharmacy, showcasing a rich history dating back centuries. The Town Hall of Malmo, a distinctive architectural gem, and Sankt Petri Kyrka (St. Peter's Church), an imposing structure with historical significance, are also within close reach.

As you meander through Stortorget Square and its surroundings, the allure of quaint restaurants and cafés beckons, providing an ideal spot to indulge in a leisurely breakfast before embarking on your journey through the city centre. This central location not only serves as a visual feast for history enthusiasts but also offers a delightful culinary experience, setting the perfect stage for a day of exploration in Malmo.

3. RIBERSBORGS KALLBADHUS BATHHOUSE

Nestled at the terminus of a pier on Ribersborg Beach, Ribersborgs Kallbadhus stands as an iconic wooden bathhouse that has been a cherished locale for locals since its establishment in 1898. This timeless institution offers a haven for recreational activities throughout the year, making it a beloved spot for residents and visitors alike.

The allure of Ribersborgs Kallbadhus lies in its diverse offerings. For those seeking aquatic enjoyment, the outdoor pools present an inviting opportunity for a refreshing swim, surrounded by the scenic beauty of Ribersborg Beach. Sunbathers can bask in the sun's warmth on the sandy shores, adding a touch of relaxation to the overall experience.

The bathhouse itself is a testament to tradition, boasting five meticulously crafted saunas. Among them, one sauna stands as a unique feature, welcoming both men and women. It's worth noting that in the saunas, an atmosphere of shared serenity is maintained, and as a customary practice, swimwear is not permitted. However, for those who may feel more comfortable, bringing towels to preserve a sense of personal space is entirely acceptable.

Ribersborgs Kallbadhus encapsulates more than a century of communal enjoyment, blending the joys of water-based activities with the therapeutic benefits of traditional saunas. Whether immersing oneself in the invigorating pools or embracing the warmth of the saunas, this historic bathhouse offers a holistic retreat, inviting patrons to partake in a timeless connection with nature and wellness.

4. **Western Harbour**

Västra Hamnen, colloquially referred to as Western Harbour, stands as a sophisticated and affluent neighbourhood, adorned with a picturesque array of oceanfront parks, charming cafés, and exquisite restaurants. Renowned for its panoramic vistas of the Øresund Bridge and the iconic Turning Torso skyscraper, this upscale enclave is a testament to modern urban planning and architectural marvels.

The crown jewel of Västra Hamnen's skyline is the Turning Torso, a residential tower soaring to a remarkable height of 190 metres. This extraordinary structure ranks among the tallest in Sweden, its distinctive feature being the topmost segment twisted 90° clockwise, creating a visual spectacle that captivates the attention of residents and visitors alike. The architectural innovation of the Turning Torso contributes to the neighbourhood's allure, defining it as a beacon of contemporary design.

Beyond the skyline, Västra Hamnen unfolds with additional attractions. The neighbourhood boasts a charming marina, providing a serene backdrop for leisurely strolls along the waterfront. Adding a touch of historical significance, a shipyard within the vicinity stands as a testament to the area's maritime heritage. Remarkably, this historic shipyard specializes in the manufacturing of submarines, blending the old-world charm of naval craftsmanship with the sleek, modern ambiance of the neighbourhood.

In essence, Västra Hamnen is more than a residential hub; it is a harmonious blend of modern luxury, breathtaking views, and maritime heritage. The coexistence of oceanfront leisure, culinary delights, and architectural wonders makes this neighbourhood a distinctive gem on the cultural map of Sweden, inviting residents and visitors alike to immerse themselves in its unique charm.

MALMO BAR CULTURE

At the southern tip of Sweden, just a Scandi-noir bridge away from Denmark, Malmö presents itself as a captivating enclave, boasting a vibrant, hospitable atmosphere that is effortlessly navigable.

As Sweden underwent industrialization and urbanization in the 19th century, the availability of industrially produced brännvin increased, contributing to escalating health and social issues related to alcohol. In response, the temperance movement gained prominence, and since 1905, the government has maintained a monopoly on the sale of liquor.

Indulging in alcohol in Sweden can be a pricey affair, but there are strategies to mitigate the cost. Opt for purchasing your drinks from the state-operated liquor stores, known as Systembolaget, instead of frequenting bars. Alternatively, explore the happy hours, often referred to as "After Work" in Swedish, offered at numerous pubs and bars.

Referred to as brännvin in Sweden, schnapps (or snaps) holds the distinction of being the country's preferred distilled liquor, crafted from potatoes or grains. Its consumption is entrenched in the Nordic country's history, particularly considering the ideal growing conditions for barley, rye, and wheat, rather than grapes.

The second most prevalent languages you are likely to encounter are Serbo-Croatian or Arabic. While English is occasionally heard, it is primarily spoken by individuals who are not fluent in Swedish. English speakers typically take longer to acquire proficiency in the language due to the widespread use of English in Sweden.

Lilla Torg square stands as the nucleus of Malmö's nightlife. For an enchanting atmosphere reminiscent of Alice in Wonderland, venture to MJ's bar and restaurant. Renowned among locals for post-work drinks, MJ's boasts a bold, playful, and colourful design.

Experience Malmö's skyline at its zenith by enjoying a cocktail at the Sky Bar, offering unparalleled views of the city's streets, squares, canals, and docks. The skilled bartenders concoct both classic and contemporary mixes, with the rum-laden Queen's Park Swizzle being a popular choice. Open Sunday-Thursday 5pm-12am, Friday 4pm-1am, and Saturday 11.30am-1am.

In Malmö's Västra Hamnen (Western Harbour), Bar Italia caters to every season. Indulge in a warm hot chocolate on chilly days or explore their extensive gelato selection, featuring unexpected flavours like whisky, for sunnier occasions. Opt for takeaway, strolling along the waterfront boardwalk with a cup or cone in hand. Open daily from 11am-8pm, extended to 10pm on Saturdays and 9pm on Sundays.

GENERAL ESSENTIAL INFORMATION

What to Do

Sauna and Swim

Extend over the chilly waters of the Öresund, the exquisitely symmetrical Ridersborgs Kallbadhus boasts a distinct Wes Anderson aesthetic. Five saunas—two female, two male, one mixed—provide warmth, while a bracing dip in the open sea offers a refreshing cool-down. Embrace the invigorating experience of the cold plunge; you may momentarily regret it, but the benefits linger throughout the day. Priced at 75kr (£6); weekdays 10 am-7 pm (8 pm on Wednesdays), weekends 9 am-6 pm.

The Strangest Museum Ever?

Upon entering the Disgusting Food Museum, receive a sick bag (your ticket) and a bingo card filled with intriguing dishes to try. Do not be discouraged; the museum showcases some of the world's most repulsive foods, offering a historical perspective on evolving food perceptions. For instance, lobster, once deemed so unpleasant it was fed to prisoners, offers hope for the acceptance of unconventional foods. Admission is 195kr (£15.50); open Wednesday to Sunday 11 am-5 pm.

Dinosaurs, for some strange reason, in a castle

Malmöhus Castle, Scandinavia's oldest preserved Renaissance castle, graces the moat-wrapped Castle Island. Home to various attractions, including the Malmö Art Museum, featuring Nordic contemporary art, and a dinosaur centre with prehistoric creature models and fossils. A visit costs 40kr (£3), covering all attractions; open daily except

Monday from 11 am-5 pm (extended to 7 pm on Thursdays).

Where to Stay

MJ's

Situated in the central Gamla Staden (old town) district, MJ's places you in the midst of the city's vibrancy. Infused with a flamingo motif and shades of green, the hotel exudes decadence with a Gatsby vibe. Black-and-gold bathroom fittings and minibar champagne add to the allure. After dark, the lobby transforms into a popular bar. Doubles from £94.

Ohboy Hotel

Recognizable by its messy green lettering, the environmentally conscious Ohboy Hotel offers functional rooms in the Västra Hamnen (Western Harbour) district. The plant-filled facade attracts butterflies and bees, watered by rain collected from the roof. Each room includes a fold-up bike for exploring the city's extensive cycle paths. Doubles from £109, room only.

Moment Hotel

A one-minute walk from the station, Moment Hotel embraces a "lean living" ethos with smaller rooms and minimal amenities. Featuring a minimalist look with bright natural colours, it serves as a stylish, affordable, and well-located base for exploration. Doubles from £80, B&B. momenthotels.com/en

Remember, when Eurovision is in town hotel prices wil vary from the norm quite dramatically!

Where to Eat

Booking ahead is advisable for a table at Aster in Malmö's regenerating docks. Set in a high-ceilinged, factory-style space, Aster cooks everything on an open flame, offering grilled octopus, lamb, and pollock accompanied by vegetables and herbs from their own farm. Open Tuesday to Thursday 5 pm-12 am, Friday to Saturday 4 pm-1 am.

Ruth's begins the day with pastries and delicious breakfast bowls and transitions to an ever-changing dinner menu. While not exactly tapas, the recommendation is to order two or three dishes per person. Open daily from 9 am-10.30 pm.

Explore, deliberate, and discover your preferences at Saluhall, a popular food hall housed in a repurposed warehouse. Units offer pizza, noodles, burgers, and curries, and deli counters provide options for take-home delights. Open weekdays 11 am-8 pm (9 pm on Fridays), weekends 11 am-5 pm.

Where to Drink

Enjoy the highest cocktail in Malmö at the Sky Bar, offering unrivalled views over the city. The bartenders craft classic and contemporary mixes, best savoured under low lighting. The rum-heavy Queen's Park Swizzle is a popular choice. Open Sunday-Thursday 5 pm-12 am, Friday 4 pm-1 am, Saturday 11.30 am-1 am.

In Västra Hamnen (Western Harbour), Bar Italia caters to the seasons with smooth hot chocolate for cooler days and a wide gelato selection, including unexpected flavours like whisky, for sunnier occasions. Opt for takeaway, strolling the waterfront boardwalk with cup or cone in hand. Open daily 11 am-8 pm, extended to 10 pm on Saturdays and 9 pm on Sundays.

Where to Shop

A 20-minute stroll south of Gamla Staden leads to Mitt Möllan, a formerly tired shopping centre transformed into a creative arcade hub. Unique stores include Möllans Te (a Chinese store selling tea and plastic toy dinosaurs), La Kasbah (Moroccan ceramics and lamps), and Beyond Retro (vintage clothing). Artists work behind glass fronts, and a central food hall offers affordable global options. Open Monday to Thursday 11 am-8 pm, Friday 11 am-9 pm, Saturday 11 am-7 pm (individual store times vary).

Architectural Highlight

Designed by Santiago Calatrava and completed in 2005, the Turning Torso stands as Scandinavia's tallest building. Resembling a twisted cheesegrater, the 54-floor residential and meeting space in Västra Hamnen serves as an architectural marvel.

The Essentials!

- - *What Currency Do I Need?* Swedish Krona.
- - *What Language Do They Speak?* Swedish, though English is widely spoken.
- - *Should I Tip?* 10 per cent in restaurants.
- - *What's the Time Difference?* One hour ahead of GMT.
- - *How Should I Get Around?* Green buses run throughout the city; tap on using your bank card at 28kr (£2) for a single ticket, double for a 24-hour pass. Most places are easily accessible on foot, or rent a bike from Travel Shop for 200kr (£16) per day.
- - *What's the Best View?* Sit on the boardwalk of Västra Hamnen at sunset, with the Öresundbron ("The Bridge" of Scandi-noir TV fame) silhouetted against the day's last light.
- - *Insider Tip?* Almost everywhere is cashless, so avoid loading up on a pile of banknotes from the ATM.

Getting There

- *Trying to Fly Less?* A new sleeper train route between Hamburg and Stockholm places Malmö within 24-hour range of London. Arrive in Malmö at 3.52 am via an early Eurostar to Brussels and onward connection to Hamburg. Day trains through Brussels, Hamburg, and Copenhagen are an alternative, with an overnight stay if not taking the sleeper.
- *Fine with Flying?* No direct flights from the UK to Malmö's airport; the nearest international airport with good UK links is Copenhagen, a 35-minute journey across a sea bridge.

Printed in Great Britain
by Amazon